MOZART
IN
PRAGUE

MOZART V PRAZE

Also by Jaroslav Seifert, from The Spirit That Moves Us:
The Casting of Bells (1983)
The Eight Days (Forthcoming: 1986)

A retrospective of Seifert, available through us:
Special edition of *The Hampden-Sydney Poetry Review* (1985)

For a complete descriptive catalogue of our publications,
write to: The Spirit That Moves Us Press, Post Office Box 1585,
Iowa City, Iowa 52244.

JAROSLAV SEIFERT

MOZART
IN
PRAGUE

THIRTEEN RONDELS

MOZART V PRAZE
Třináct Rondels

BILINGUAL EDITION
With Translation from the Czech by
Paul Jagasich and Tom O'Grady

THE SPIRIT THAT MOVES US PRESS: IOWA CITY
1985

Cover design and illustration by Richard McClintock.
Photograph on back cover by Miroslav Jodas.
Typesetting and mechanical preparation courtesy of Hampden-
Sydney College Publications Office.

Library of Congress Cataloging in Publication Data:

Seifert, Jaroslav, 1901-
    Mozart in Prague

    1. Mozart, Wolfgang Amadeus, 1756-1791—Poetry.
I. Title.   II. Title: Mozart v Praze.
PG5038.S45M613 1985   891.8'615   85-11907
ISBN 0-930370-27-9 (pbk.)

Translators' Note

We include the Czech and English versions of these brief poems not for comparisons of similarities but so that the reader, if he is capable in both languages, may note the differences. As the well-known Czechoslovakian poet Miroslav Holub points out, "Seifert's early poetry, because of his emphasis on devices of sound and musical technique, is virtually untranslatable. The best we can hope to do, those of us trying to bring him into English, is to create an equivalent poem that reads well in the current tongue." Indeed, the English here is intended as a copy of the original only to the extent that we have tried to capture the spirit of the Czech language while keeping the rondel form. A translation which is too literal might not bring over the form, and one that succumbs to the demands of form alone might lose something of the spontaneous and the unpredictable aspects which are so much a part of Jaroslav Seifert's poetry. But form is obviously at the center of these little dances, and so lines were shaped and turned where necessary to keep within the pattern—but never so much, we hope, as to take us entirely away from the meaning, the intent, or the grace of these tightly constructed poems.

Paul Jagasich and Tom O'Grady
Hampden-Sydney, Virginia
Spring 1985

I.

Kdybych na flétnu uměl hrát,
tak jako umím verše s rýmy!
Nač slova? Co si počne s nimi
ta, keteré chce se tancovat,

zaslechne-li jen vítr vát
v soumračném tichu dlouhé zimy?
Kdybych na flétnu uměl hrát,
tak jako umím verše s rýmy!

Jdu hledat hrob. Za mříží vrat
je tma už a snad zavřeli mi.
Ne, ještě ne! Zůstal jsem stát,
šeptaje si tu před mrtvými:

Kdybych na flétnu uměl hrát!

I.

I'd like to play a singing flute,
while these poems are rimed in place!
She wants nothing but a dance,
for her the words are brutal,

and the cold wind rants at the hooded
windows, the dark season's forgotten
 face.
I'd like to play a singing flute,
while these poems are rimed in place!

I look for a grave. Fog covers the route.
Gates close behind me, a hand of grace.
No, not yet! Here I stay, my boots
halt as the dead whisper, white and
 chaste.

I'd like to play a singing flute!

II.

Co zbývá tu z přízraku már,
jež vcházely pod nízkou bránu?
Nic. Trochu vody na břečťanu,
jenž vrůstává až na dno spár.

A to, co poznamenal zmar,
je oblečeno v tarlatánu.
Co zbývá tu z přízraku már,
jež vcházely pod nízkou bránu?

A mrtvi? Jenom křížů pár
teď sklání se v tu onu stranu,
zatímco anděl zdusil žár
své pochodně o chladnou hranu.

Co zbývá tu z přízraku már?

II.

What remains of vanity's ghosts,
gone under a low arcade?
Nothing. Puddles of water, ivy laid,
stand in crevices and glow.

And that which ruins richly host,
is covered with a heavy brocade.
What remains of vanity's ghosts,
gone under a low arcade?

And the dead? Two crosses at most
leaning toward one another fade,
while an angel's flame rises like a rose
and his torch warms the rounding
   shade.

What remains of vanity's ghosts?

III.

Chci vzbudit mrtvou, jít jí vstříc,
i kdyby sto let mrtva byla
a u zdi se mi objevila
jak stín, jejž na zeď vrhá nic.

Chci spatřit její vlas i líc
a oči, vše, co smrt už smyla,
chci vzbudit mrtvou, jít jí vstříc,
i kdyby sto let mrtva byla.

Sto let a třeba ještě víc,
jen kdybych věděl, kde se skryla
a v ševel listí, zpívajíc,
svá ústa dávno proměnila;

chci vzbudit mrtvou, jít jí vstříc.

III.

Let the woman rise, I'll follow,
one hundred years from her death.
Let the shadow appear, let her breath
shiver against these walls, meek and
    shallow.

I want to see her hair, her face in its
    hollows,
and the eyes: all that time has sheathed.
Let the woman rise, I'll follow,
one hundred years from her death.

One hundred years and more, mellowed
in the grey corners where she lies
    beneath
the breath of a song on lips burrowed
in the clasp of a single leaf.

Let the woman rise, I'll follow.

IV.

Už kolem všechno zavál čas
a nikdo z živých nevzpomíná,
zapomněla i sama hlína,
kde zasypán byl její hlas,

a nikdo nepřináší vzkaz,
kde leží mrtvá Josefína;
už kolem všechno zavál čas
a nikdo z živých nevzpomíná.

Já vzpomněl si však na obraz:
zrávaly jste tu, hrozny vína,
a ten, jenž tenkrát trhal vás,
myslil na ústa milenčina;

ůz kolem všechno zavál čas.

IV.

Time has engulfed everything around
  here,
no one living remembers.
Even Earth herself cannot read the
  embers
where her voice has been seared.

And no one will ever draw us near
to tell where our dead Josefina lingers.
Time has engulfed everything around
  here,
no one living remembers.

Yet I recall one lovely year,
alone in a garden where grapevines
  rendered
their fruit to my lips, just near
her remembered eyes, and I sent for her.

Time has engulfed everything around
  here.

V.

Čas všude kreslí nehtem zlým,
a dešť ty čáry v maltě drolí.
Vidím v nich záliv v Neapoli,
moře a sopku, nad ní dým.

A vinice, blízko je Řím,
tam květů je, až hlava bolí.
Čas všude kreslí nehtem zlým,
a dešť ty čáry v maltě drolí.

— Tu píseň? Možná. Uvidím!
Však hostitelka nepovolí.
Dnes to tu dýchá chladem zim.
Podíváš-li se na cokoli,

čas všude kreslí nehtem zlým.

V.

The wicked claws of time scar enough,
and rain mixes magic with mortar.
In the Bay of Naples, strange order:
sea, volcano and smoke above.

In the vineyards near Rome, flowers
    shudder,
trying the mind's borders.
The wicked claws of time scar enough,
and rain mixes magic with mortar.

But to write songs here? Perhaps. The
    doves
fly, our keeper protects her larder.
When the cold wind cuts quick to love,
you will notice small sins, not slaughter.

The wicked claws of time scar enough.

VI.

Addio, krásný plameni!
Nápěv se lehce dotkl čela
a ta, jíž patřil, zamlčela
to, co je k nevyslovení.

Nerozsvěcejte! Při stmění
slova se nezdají tak smělá.
Addio, krásný plameni,
nápěv se lehce dotkl čela.

A oba byli zmateni.
Z rozpaků okno otevřela.
Svit noci padal na denní
a v dálce Praha zrůžověla.

Addio, krásný plameni!

VI.

Beautiful love flames—goodbye!
Music touches me like a gentle finger.
And she, the lonely singer,
will not talk of the unspeakable lie.

Put out the light! In the dark, the eye
knows the weak words that linger here.
Beautiful love flames—goodbye!
Music touches me like a gentle finger.

Both of us become confused and shy.
A window slowly opens on the shimmer
of night battling with the rising sky.
Prague, far away, is rosy pink and
   glimmers.

Beautiful love flames—goodbye!

VII.

Řeknu-li Praha, běda mi,
hned vaše oči zazáří mně;
jako bych shodil s ramen břímě
vždy pod těmito střechami.

A nestojím-li před vámi,
vše kolem zní tak neupřímně.
Řeknu-li Praham, běda mi,
hned vaše oči zazáří mně.

Budu se vracet neznámý
a chudý, třeba v dešti, v zimě,
a v koutku lůžko ze slámy
bych nezměnil za palác v Římě.

Řeknu-li Praha, běda mi!

VII.

I will never say I'm sorry, Prague,
so long as your eyes shine on me.
Each time I sleep under these roofs, a
     sea,
my shoulders lighten in the heavy fog.

Am I a stranger from the sodden bogs,
or the one before you that you see?
I will never say I'm sorry, Prague,
so long as your eyes shine on me.

If ever I return, unknown and sogging
in the snow, my straw mat full of fleas,
give me a rough floor of logs
and not a Roman villa ushered by
     decree.

I will never say I'm sorry, Prague.

VIII.

Nechtělo se mu vyjet z bran,
byl unaven však z toho shonu.
Praha je plná jeho tónů
jak čerstvě orosený džbán.

Snad přijde opět šedý pán,
má před očima již tvář onu;
nechtělo se mu vyjet z bran,
byl unaven však z toho shonu.

Zavalen kufry ze všech stran,
schoulil se mlčky za záclonu
a jeli. Jako rány hran
zněly mu tenkrát hlasy zvonů;

nechtělo se mu vyjet z bran.

VIII.

He left these gates, dazed,
as if too tired of the chase.
Prague, full of his colors, gracefully
stood like a freshly painted vase.

He'll come again, greyhaired and
    amazed.
And I will see nothing but his face.
He left these gates, dazed,
as if too tired of the chase.

While he waited in those glazed
Rooms, the curtains swayed; their lace,
full of light, the suitcases piled outside
    in the hazy
morning, and the bells sang to him: an
    echo, a face.

He left these gates, dazed.

IX.

Šel pohřeb, mrtvý byl tak sám.
A Vídeň? Tančí bez oddechu.
Pohřbívali ho jenom v spěchu,
vždyť nevědí dnes ani kam.

A tanec šumí. Nožky dam
nic nezadrží při poslechu.
Šel pohřeb, mrtvý byl tak sám.
A Vídeň? Tančí bez oddechu.

Smutek a ticho lehly tam,
kde nacházel vždy vlídnou střechu.
Znáš pražské zvony? Znám je, znám
a poslouchám je pro útěchu.

Šel pohřeb, mrtvý byl tak sám.

IX.

Begin the funeral; the body is lonely.
And Vienna dances breathlessly.
Somewhere at a poor grave a stranger
    restlessly
places the one that is now his only.

How can they make of their swirling,
    such glory?
The delicate quick feet of the women
    flash noiselessly.
Begin the funeral; the body is lonely.
And Vienna dances breathlessly.

Both silence and sorrow cry in the heart
    alone,
and the friendly canopy of roofs seems
    to fold helplessly.
Do you know the bells of Prague? The
    groaning
and thrashing sing deathlessly.

Begin the funeral; the body is lonely.

X.

Tak umí umřít jenom pták
a padá střemhlav v rosu trávy.
Vždyť nikdo o tom nevypráví,
nevědí ani kdy a jak.

Možná, že padal do oblak
jak plamen rozžhavené lávy.
Tak umí umřít jenom pták
a padá střemhlav v rosu trávy.

A s žebráky jak lidský vrak
šat z hlíny měl jen popelavý,
když prošel tmou a vcházel pak
už přímo do světel a slávy.

Tak umí umřít jenom pták.

X.

Only a bird knows how to die:
falling on to dew-filled grass headfirst.
But we don't care, we don't cry, we
    thirst
for the moment when we're told if it's
    death or birth.

We rise in volcanic flames to the high
bursts of clouds and we are lost.
Only a bird knows how to die:
falling on to dew-filled grass headfirst.

We may come with the lowest beggars
    of our kind
covered in the ash-grey shades of our
    clay dresses.
But we will rush through mist and fog
    and fly
straight to the shining light that hides
    the curse.

Only a bird knows how to die.

XI.

Však začnem jinou, není spěch,
ač zazněl z hodin úder trojí.
A zrcadlo se vždycky bojí,
když někdo stoupá po schodech.

Zpěvák, jenž k písni nabral dech,
teď mlčí; škoda nebylo jí,
však začnem jinou, není spěch,
ač zazněl z hodin úder trojí.

Co bylo písní v těchto zdech,
teď je tu vše jak pod závoji.
A ten, jenž spával na hroznech,
bloudí tu ještě po pokoji,

však začnem jinou, není spěch.

XI.
Let's begin again like green spring, but
  don't hurry.
Wait until the clock strikes three.
We always see fear in the mirrors
and we climb the steps unsteadily.

The poet who breathed only to sing has
  no worries.
He's silent now like a folded leaf.
Let's begin again like green spring, but
  don't hurry.
Wait until the clock strikes three.

All that came from that breath now lies
  in the murky
shadows of the corners, covered with a
  veil of grief.
In the wine cellars he sang of fury
and content—now he is a blind pigeon
  in the eaves.

Let's begin again like green spring, but
  don't hurry.

XII.

Pár zkřehlých ptáků ve větvích
slétne se někdy k jeho jménu.
Vyrvali révu do kořenů
a mělkou studnu zavál sníh.

Bratříček jejich, jeden z nich,
hrával jim z okna kantilénu,
pár zkřehlých ptáků ve větvích
slétne se nědky k jeho jménu.

Strop, který slyšel šťastný smích,
řekl si jednou: Zapomenu.
Vešlo tam prázdno a dům ztich,
dnes skrývá se tu za ozvěnu

pár zkřehlých ptáků ve větvích.

XII.

Two frozen birds touch bare branches,
drawn here quivering at his call.
The grapes are clawed away, the seeds
    fall,
the deep ponds are buried as the snow
    advances.

The little brother is one of them, and he
    launches
into song, his voice at the window,
    gentle and small.
Two frozen birds touch bare branches,
drawn here quivering at his call.

The ceiling above still hears the
    laughter, its arches
speaking out in remembrance as the
    sounds rise and fall.
And the silence within, the hollow that
    embraces
everything with a velvet echo, covers
    like a warm shawl.

Two frozen birds touch bare branches.

XIII.

Mé verše jsou však z olova,
toužil jsem marně po té Múze,
jdu za ní, ale ke své hrůze
civím zas u bran hřbitova.

Bojím se, zda se neschová
mým očím v sedmibarvé duze,
mé verše jsou však z olova,
toužil jsem marně po té Múze.

Prchá mi noha růžová,
dívám se jen, jak po zásluze
se vznáší k nebi, nad slova,
až tam, kde krok už není chůze;

mé verše jsou však z olova.

XIII.
My poems are heavy, like molded lead,
from this desperate longing after the
  Muse.
I'll stand with her before the threaten-
  ing truths,
and I will stare, suddenly, at the gates of
  the dead.

Forgive me, but my eyes become suffused
with the seven-colored light the rainbow
  sheds.
My poems are heavy, like molded lead,
from this desperate longing after the
  Muse.

My wrapped pink foot carries me
  quickly ahead,
and my eyes glance, always, after writing
  sad news
to those skies beyond the word said
where our steps carry the heart alone
  and bruised.

My poems are heavy, like molded lead.